Pieces
of
My Soul

Vol. 1
"A Collection of Poetic Expressions"

By: Terron D. Wilkerson

DIVINE HOUSE BOOKS

About The Author

Terron D. Wilkerson began writing poetry at the age of 23 during his time abroad in Ghana. However, it truly began upon his eviction from the womb December 1, 1991 in Millington, Tennessee. Terron has since been referred to through a variety of aliases: Bear, Tee, Sauce and Kwesi, to name a few. Although he only wishes to be known by one, The Greatest Scribe Alive, under the strict stipulation his title is earned, not given. He currently resides where the stars do not shine, but it is sunny every day, with his Dalmatian, Spot and 1985 DeLorean.

Acknowledgment

I dedicate this collection to the Universe for introducing the right people, places and opportunities into my life from which I derive the inspiration for my dreams to manifest.

Table of Contents

Hey, Pops

Hey, Pops
I wrote this one for you
The day I was born you had a dream
Now it's finally coming true
Remember feeding me that jalapeño pepper
When I was 4
& watching my face go askew?
Or just wasting time at Camp...
"Whatever" every summer?
Because believe me, I do

But that was all a long time
Before I turned 22
The day of MY dreams at graduation
Became a nightmare
I never meant to hurt you Pops
That's my word, I swear
But before I get too deep
Let me not take it there
Because I still recall the good times
Like the pretty Asian lady
You let cut my hair

So many precious jewels
Bagged up in a third of my life
Including some imperfect diamonds
That still cause me strife
Like fighting back the tears
Every time I was forced to take flight
On my return trips to hell

Locked in solitary
For 17 years
No chance to post bail

Lately I've cried
Recalling the pain
She put me through
I cry even harder
When I realize
What she did to you
But those same memories of you
Always helped me pull through
I swear I recall them so well...

Like the time I ate just a plain tortilla
Out of the microwave
& you laughed until your mouth turned stale
I swear I recall them so well

Father & son
Just the two of us
So young, so innocent, so sincere
It still drives me wild
You're turning 50 this year
I know you were a young man once
& although you may disagree
We have so much in common
Because when I look into your eyes,
I see visions of me

You taught me
I can be a man & still cry
You taught me

How to treat a woman right
& most importantly,
You taught me how to fly
Because of those lessons
My wings have just reached
An all-time high

You see, there's no way
I can ever pay you back
But I will send your ashes to the moon
Like you always wanted
I promise you that
Might even get you that hover-round
With the decked out rims
But in the meantime,
In between time, our time spent
Will no longer be fresh fruit
Hanging from a broken stem

Sometimes I find myself wishing
I could go back in time
& do it all again
Escape solitary for good
& forever call you my best friend
But a great man also taught me
There's a reason every story
Must come to an end
So I'm officially closing that chapter
To allow our new one, to begin.

Sunshine & Rain

They say, "All's fair
In love & war"
If that's true, then let's take a
Walk down memory lane
While I tell you about this girl

See, if her beauty had a scene
It would gleam... like the rays
Of an autumn sunset
If her beauty had charm
It would resemble the first time
You held a baby in your arms
If her beauty had style
It would be like sitting
In front of a blank canvas
& just painting... for a while

If her beauty had power
It would be fierce enough to
Wrestle Deebo into submission
You see, the girl was bad
& not bad meaning bad,
But bad meaning... flawless

Unfortunately, she was also
Bad meaning bad
Cruella de Vil to be exact
Bad for me, bad for we, bad for

Helping me to keep such a
Beautiful picture, intact

One day she asked me,
"Tee, how deep is your love?"
I told her, "Baby, not all things can be
Measured with a ruler.
But if you loved me just as deep,
It might make our hot situation
A bit cooler"

It seemed as if my steady persistence
Pushed her further over the cliff
Into her depths of indifference
I even let her set the terms
For the remainder of our coexistence

Smooth criminal
Used to be one myself,
So I can't complain
But this time you
Stole MY heart
& moonwalked out of MY life
Before I even had a chance
To ask your name

A happy memory escapes
With each fallen tear
Until your presence
Is no longer here (mind)...
Or here (heart)

Regardless, I know the next girl I'm with
Will be so much BADDER than you
Or maybe that's just what I tell myself
So I can pull through
Nowadays I can't help but wonder if
When you're alone,
Do you think of me too?
Because all I have left is
A broken heart
& these reminiscent words
For now... that will have to do.

Fi(Hom)e

At night, when I'm alone
I close my eyes
& I zone
Simultaneously
I see visions of me
Traveling the long road
Home

But what is home?

Some may say
The place one can roam
The place shaped like a lopsided cone
The place of rain forests & sandstorms
The place I am obligated to adorn

Others may say
The place your physique is honed
The place leisure overflows like foam
The place hate runs through you like a comb
The place fear controls you like a drone

I say otherwise
But needless to say
I'll never know my true home
Anyway.

Coretta Scott-Queen

I wrote this one for the Queens
Black women
The coffee to my cream
Black women
The engine to my steam
Black women
The physical manifestation
Of my dreams
Black women
I'm about to get deep
Please, follow what I mean

It's such a shame
That because of the way
Your skin gleams
The world shuns you
& isn't always what it seems
But you've survived through it all
Reclaiming your ancestral royalty
& I'm so, so inspired
By how your
Chocolate soul beams

No need to feel alone
I know what the world did to you
My own mother is light-skinned
I know what master did too

On behalf of Black men
I must apologize
For our misguided rage,
Reckless mistakes,
& betraying lies
Nothing will be the same
The day we finally realize
The key to our liberation
Is hidden between those
Pretty brown eyes

& since we're being honest
The fruits of true pleasure
Take root between those
Pretty brown thighs

But please,
Don't misinterpret my intent
I can call a spade a spade
Without provoking
Any disrespect
Mama raised me
To be a gentleman
& she'll STILL
Snatch me up by my neck!
But enough about that
Let's get back to the topic...

If our ancestors saw you today
I know they'd be proud
Your existence is an inspiration

With the sole purpose to astound
I'll worship you 'til the day I die
With my head, feet AND pride
To the ground
Because you remind me of the days
When James Brown told us to
SAY IT LOUD!

I love the way you
Make me feel
I love the way you've
Allowed me to heal
I love the ambition
In your eyes
I love the potential
We have to rise... together

We've been through the storm
Meaning we can survive
Any weather... together
They treat us like rats
But that won't stop us from
Getting to the cheddar... together
Love & unity are the only way
So let's join hands & pave
A new road for our generation
Today... together.

Slave to Modesty

Delivery smooth as ice
I hope my content is hot enough
To keep you from freezing
Even Jesus put away the games
When he came of age
So, no need for the teasing
My confidence, poise, stature
All so appeasing
I can see your walls coming down
Hopefully not just, for those reasons

Your appetite for me
Is insatiable
My desire for you
Is irreplaceable
The sound of your heartbeat
Is unmistakable
Accelerating, accelerating, accelerating
...like somebody is chasing you

Or maybe you're just on the run
From how you really feel
I have some medicine for you
In these words
So open up your eyes
& allow your body, to heal

Trust me, I'm a professional
Now allow us to fly
I'll be your pilot for the evening
No need to ask why

Fair warning:
You may experience
Shortness of breath
At such high altitudes
Fortunately, I plan to exchange
More than just oxygen
With you

I don't know how much
Longer you can wait
By the look in your eyes
I see you getting impa...tient
In heavy anticipation
Of this ela...tion
So far you've only seen a glimpse
Of my determina...tion
Baby, just wait until I see you naked

But in the meantime
I'd prefer to keep
Stroking your mind
To see how much deeper
I can take...it

If these walls could talk
They might say it was a murder
Your 'moan'ologues

So loud & artistic
Placing a new mural
On each
& every
Corner

Maybe that's because
I can taste fresh pineapple
On my tongue
& it seems to make you feel alright
Funny thing is,
There isn't a fruit stand in sight

But with these words
I'll continue to incite
In hopes that your lust
Continues to burn bright
In hopes that soon
You'll feel, more than alright
So sit back, relax
& allow me
To take control...
Tonight.

I Walked to the Otherside of the World
to Find a Clean Washroom

Nonsense, nonsense
Hop skip
Hulk leap
Lukewarm porridge

Hibernation slumber
Sanity buried in storage
Food doesn't feel the same
Anymore

Vampires invaded my
Mosquito net at 4am
The apocalypse is near

A rooster's crow abducts me
From my sweet escape
Although my eyes never closed

Never use the washroom stall
Furthest from the entry
It's a trap

Imagine if John Lennon
Never created "Imagine"
Imagine if Elvis Presley
Wasn't such a prick

Even felines don't always
Land on their feet

It's ironic
How desirable white women
Feel in Africa
When they must cloak themselves
With western medicine
To persuade their skin
From melting

The second bowl of hookah
Never tastes as good

How can one write about heartbreak
When one's never been in love?
How can one write about, lust
When one's never know the moistness
Of her insides?
Is there such a thing as
Too many white lies?

It shocks me that I still
Emulate my father this much
After 23 years
It seems somehow,
Emasculating...
Whatever.

El Guapo Cinco

My journey didn't really start
Until I got to college
Best memories of my life
On the pursuit of happiness
& knowledge

Met a group of young princes
Aspiring to be kings
Refusing to settle for less
The fruition of a King's dream

We've come a long way
Since swimming in pools of E&J
Partying all night,
Pretending to study all day

Re-introduced the real to campus
By showing them apples vs. oranges
Started from the bottom
Like a mediocre chorus
Some would say it was fate
Others hocus pocus
All I know is we left our mark
& all it took was focus

I remember my intervention
In Doc's lab on the 3rd floor
If y'all weren't my brothers

I'd for sure have to settle that score
But it made me a better man
Gave me a better plan...
Of action, now
"May no man alive come through
& damage my faction"

Even if I wanted new friends
The universe couldn't provide better ones
The world isn't ready
For what we have to teach our sons.

noitcelfeReflection

Depression is a hell of a drug

Critiquing my imperfections
In a restaurant mirror
Gorging myself on the traits
That other people admire
Blue flames beneath my misery
Slowly melt the smile from my face
Into a vat of blackened sentiments
It's warm inside
Satan's womb

Was I born like this?
Or just reborn into it?
Lingering pain dictates my existence
Like the village elder
Of my broken psyche
There is no escape
When the enemy is your own shadow
& it is always 12pm

My insides gush blood
With no external wound in sight
Over-consumption has always been
My greatest vice

Even Tom Cruise would be crippled
By the mission impossible I've inherited

To fill the hole in my soul

Tried to fill the hole in my soul
With things so unnatural
But my body regurgitated it
Like poisoned food
Except the food I can no longer stomach
Is happiness

But what's the point of having
A whole soul without holes, anyhow?
Why feel in a world with no emotion?
Why heal when we have ethanol potions?
Why try & deal in matters of the heart
When we've already been dealt our cards
From the start?
At least these recollections
Used to be bittersweet
Now they're just tart.

Madre

Loving you is complicated
All these years later
& I haven't gotten any closer to
Peace of mind

But if you ever need
A new heart
Rest assured
I'd give you a
Piece of mine

& in a way,
You kind of do
Or kind of did
But a lot has changed
Since I was a kid

Not every hatchet can be
Buried & forgotten
But I swear to you
That won't
Stop me from trying

Just the thought
Of whether... or not
You loved me... or not
Still keeps me up...
At night

Because it hurts so bad
It doesn't help that
My father claims
I'm cursed
To date hurt... women
The rest of MY life
Because of OUR relationship
But I don't listen to him anymore
Or at least, not as much as I did
Because a lot has changed
Since I was a kid

Even after all the scars
I still feel the need
To apologize
Because I'll never truly know
If it was my father you saw
When you looked in my eyes
Even after all the scars
I still feel the need
To apologize
Because I'll never truly know
If you ever loved me,
At least until recently

But you did a great job
Marrying my step dad
He's a real good man

& you did a great job
Teaching me
Everything I know

Because everything I know
Has gotten me very far
You never dimmed my light
& always allowed me to be a star
I'll never forget how proud you were
In 5th grade
When I gave that speech
For grandpa

One day,
Someday soon,
I want to know
Who you were
Before I came to know
Who you are
But every time I try
It's awkward
So maybe later

But please,
Don't take these
Words out of context
I love you, mama
& that becomes easier to admit
The more our Communication
becomes solid

So rest assured with the, knowledge
Our journey is far from over
The only difference is
This time,
I'm not afraid of the ride.

Tattered Yellow Notebook

3 water bottles
All lined in a row
1 empty, 1 full
1 opened
Quite some time ago

I see trash on the ground
But not regular trash
The kind of trash
That never ends up
In a can

I wonder how the ocean
Feels today
Atlantic is her name
Those without understanding
Look at her & see
Business all the same

But I look at Atlantic
With marvel in my eyes
Because every day she has
To offer
Is a brand new
Surprise
& don't get me started
On her best friend,
The skies

When the sun sets
They're butternut hazel
Like her pretty brown eyes
Never imagined she'd be
The one
To cut me down to size.

The Girl of My Dreams

I saw you today
Well, more like
I saw you walking away
Even if I wanted to
I wouldn't know
What else to say

But let me take you back
To the beginning
I believe it was a Monday
But not like that matters
Because all I remember
Is your motherfucking face

Two seconds of eye contact
Felt like an eternity
Who would've thought?
You'd end up
Changing my destiny?
We connected
At the height of my depression
Felt like the universe
Was testing me
But you helped me through it
& turned my world
Upside down
Like a comma
To an apostrophe

You taught me I can love again
My past girlfriends would tell you
I'm a scrub
So that's mission impossible
But all it took was some TLC
In the International Students' Hostel

But in the end, letting you in
Gave me a bad case of "the sads"
Now all I listen to is "Bad Religion"
& "U Got It Bad"

The closer we got
The more obscure things seemed
I can't believe you used to be
The girl of my dreams.

One Last Dance

Yesterday was quite bittersweet
Spent the whole day together
Without dispute
What a feat!
Well, for us at least

But you still managed
To cramp my style
Like new shoes
Too small for my feet

I made sure you
Wanted for nothing
So you ended up
Just wanting to hurt me

It hurts to realize
My love wasn't worth it
Boiling pot of epiphanies
Bubbling over the surface

You cared more about
Your depiction
Than changing our reality
Can't even share a meal with you
In fear you might poison my food
With your internal treachery

I truly hope you figure things out
Before hurting someone
You actually care about
If I said this was about you
I know you'd still have doubts
Then again, knowing you
You'd hear me out
If I chose to shout

I was a fool to
Expect you to know strength
When this entire time
You've mistaken my kindness
For weakness
Just thinking about it
Makes me sick to my stomach.

Alomo Bitters

Thought I could pretend
But this is much more fun
From the very beginning
I thought you would be my
Beautiful One
I thought we'd end in matrimony
Before our chapter was done
But it turns out girls really do
Just want to have fun

Yea, my feelings got hurt
But I'm not stressing
Next time I'll take notes
When the universe tries
To teach me a lesson
But as for you & I,
A peaceful reunion?
I'd rather swallow
A hearty spoonful of resin

Hahahaha
Wait wait, don't walk away
I'm just playing
But all good jokes contain truth, shit
My conscience tried to warn me
But instead you hung me
With the same rope I tried
To hold us together with

Should've seen it from the beginning
With Rudy Francisco
Your admiration for him hit me
Like a torpedo to my heart
Shouldn't have been so cheap
& actually paid attention
Or opened my eyes
From the very start

Because when you try hard,
That's when you die hard
Now my homies interrogating me
Like, "Why Sauce?!"
When I tell them that I fell for you
My Goddddd.

Broken Promises

I really wish
I didn't
Fucking hate you
Then it wouldn't be
So hard to admit
I used to
Fucking date you
I really wish
I didn't
Fucking hate you
Then it wouldn't be
So hard to admit
I still
Fucking love you

I look forward
To the day
I'm able to
Look you in the eyes
Without fucking flinching
I look forward
To the day
I'm able to
Say your name
Without fucking hesitation
I look forward
To the day
I'm able to

Scroll past your pic
On Instagram
Without fucking staring
I look forward
To the day
I'm able to
Read our old texts
Without fucking crying

But I can't
Look forward to anything
Until I can stop
Looking back
At you.

Gil Scott-Hearin'

Quite often lately
My colleagues have been
Questioning me
Dissecting me
Asking, "Tee...
Are you ready to go home?"
To most I lie
But I tell the truth to some
As in response, I ask them,
"How do I answer when I don't
Have a home to go back to?"
Or, "How do you call
Somewhere 'home'
When it's obvious...
Your family doesn't love you?"

What hurts even worse
Is looking my Ghanaian friends
In the eyes
& telling them nothing but
Good-intentioned lies
Because when they ask
About me, returning
I really want to say,
"The way things are at 'home'
This Native Son may not
Make it back alive, anyway"

I used to be afraid of the dark
Which I'm not ashamed to admit
But what can be more frightening
Than how afraid I've been made
Of my own Black skin?

I used to be ashamed of this skin
Which I am ashamed to admit
Even at 12 years old
I couldn't believe I'd been cursed
With such a dark life sentence

America never really wanted
To let go of her... niggers
Kidnapped me from my Mother
& history hasn't been the same since

& if I'm so "free" now
Then why does my history
Start with slavery
& the rest still neglect-ed?
As if nothing mattered prior to
European con-tact
Now ain't that some shit?

It's ironic how
You wouldn't teach me
Your religion

Because you said
I had no soul
Until you convinced me
It was a fair trade to exchange
My rebellious soul
For your pacifying bible
600 years later & we're still
Wash, rinse, repeating
The same cycle

It's ironic how
You talk about
The Jewish Holocaust
Like the greatest crime
Against humanity
But what about
My Holocaust
& the crimes you committed
During slavery?
I see the shame in your eyes
But what's even sadder to see
Is how you never
Want to discuss it
When we have company

But the truth shall set you free!
I know what you think of me
Don't waste my time with lies
Thug nigger, drug dealer
I see the look of disgust in your eyes

Same reason the Ku Klux Kongress
Won't let Obama get a bill through
Because they'd rather
Watch America crumble
Than let a nigger
Tell them what to do...

& speaking of which
It makes me sick seeing
Black-skinned Negropeans
With British accents
Wearing western fashions
Emulating the oppressor
Ultimate culture clashing
Spitting in the face
Of our forcefully forgotten past,
&...

Black-skinned overseers
In sheep's clothing
Preaching to us
"Progress is a marathon,
Not a sprint"
Meanwhile, the train already left
& all my white friends
Were already on it
Now ain't THAT some shit?!

Fortunately, a King named Martín
Taught me to sacrifice my life
For the beat

But I don't mean the kind of beat that
Has you moving your feet
I mean the kind of beat that
Enlivens my people in the streets
I mean the kind of beat that
Inspires my brothers & sisters
Sleeping under prison sheets
I mean the kind of beat that
Invigorated the souls in 400 years
Of enslaved human beings

& to my heroes in
Ferguson, Baltimore, The Bay
& beyond
I see you grooving
To that same beat,
No disguise
I'll be home soon & I hope
My new shade of Black is
An ABOMINATION
In America's eyes

Assata taught me
We have nothing to lose but our chains
So long as we keep hope alive,
We can continue to pave a NEW
Revolutionary Road... starting TODAY,
BECAUSE STILL WE RISE.

New Millennium, Old Struggle

Tupac had to die
If he lived it wouldn't be right
Just another Black leader
For us to fight &
Eventually despise

Sometimes I wonder,
Does Obama cry at night?

Die a hero
Or live long enough to
Become a villain

Big heap of self-hate
Piled on top of
The dead bodies
From multigenerational
Race-based killings.

B & E

The house alarm shrieks
Pumping distress signals
Into the veins
Of your empty hallways
You have not awoken

Glass shatters
& hurried footsteps follow
Warning the curtains
Of ensuing danger
You have not awoken

Your bedroom door gyrates
But does not give
At least the lock
Is putting up a fight
You have not awoken

Thump...
Thump....
THUMP.....
PSHHHHH!!!
The sound of splintering wood
Can easily be mistaken
For the breaking of bones
You have not awoken

A solid gold Desert Eagle
Is aimed at the
Entrance to your soul
It's like that moment when
Everyone knows what will happen
Except the person being cheated on

You have not awoken
Frustratingly the invader
Pulls you out of bed
Only to find
That you are already dead.

Trauma

What's up Doc?
You've been my best friend
Since as far back
As I can remember
Strangely enough,
I don't remember much
From before freshman year
But rewind to 2013
& I'll always remember
The piece you performed
At Black Grad
& every happy tear

Looking back even further
It's hard to encompass
6 years
In just a few verses
But I'll always remember
You being the first one
To give me true courage
When I was barely twen-ty
You pulled me aside & told me,
"Tee, you have to learn
To let people in"
But I didn't listen to you
The 1st time
Or even the 27th

Now rewind to 2011
When they kicked me
Out of school &
Set fire to my safe haven
You gave me
Some pocket money
& a safe place to stay in
Even as I fought my way back
You were with me
Every step of the way
It's memories like those that
Solidify our friendship
Every single day

Now fast forward to 2015
As I'm gracing Ghana's stage
Trying to capture the dream
I've been sold,
Telling my story to the world,
But lo & behold, I'm still
Afraid to tell these stories
To the bros
Mainly because most of them
Have never seen
This side of me... before
Well, that & the fact
I have a bad reputation
For stepping on
Other people's toes

I mean...
Laying down lyrics
Was always your thing
Making it big
Was always your dream
Now every time I
Pick up my pen to write
I feel like I'm
Burning a new hole...
In your wings.

Hey love,
Do you remember the
First time we kissed?
Overlooking the safari in Mole
That's a moment I'll forever miss

We started making love
The first week we met
But that's what happens
When 2 souls that are
Destined to meet
Finally connect...
There's no shame in that

But baby girl,
It didn't take long
To catch your drift
You never wanted love
You just wanted
To hold all the chips

That's the same selfishness
That ruined our relationship
I'd be lying to both of us
If I said, "No hard feelings"

You dug a grave &
Made reservations for 2
But finally I realized
It would be emotional suicide
Continuing to lay with you
There was a time in my life
When I would've done ANYTHING
Just to stay with you
But you let go of the rope
& forced me to bid you adieu
They already told me
That's not the story you tell
Whenever they ask you
Maybe that's because,
You forgot too

Anyway, I promised myself
This is the last time
I'll ever write about you...
But I'll always wonder
What I could've done
To be more adored like Rudy
Maybe I should've made comments
That were just less snobby
I hope one day you can
Patch things up with your daddy

Because until then, a good man
Will never make you happy.
Hey Pops,
It's me again
Still reflecting on the times
When YOU were my best friend
Still reflecting on the times
When I was just YOUR little man
Still reflecting on the times
When you would've given ME
A second chance
But frankly, lately I feel like...
You just don't give a damn

I can tell a million stories
About how things used to be
If you ever want to read them
Take a look at my first poetry
But if you ever read this, I know
That's not what you'll want to see
Because in all honesty, I have
No idea how to make you happy

Why is it so hard to open up &
Just tell me what I did wrong?
When did it become so easy for me
To vent about you in a sad song?
Never thought I'd see the day
Where I see you like
I used to see my mom
Especially when you used to be

My everyday Superman
Saving my sanity all along
Where did you go?!
I need my invincible,
Unconditional loving father back
I won't apologize
Because there ain't no way
I can soften that
It's gotten to the point where
I feel more comfortable
Writing about you than
Writing you a WhatsApp
Now I'll forever know the difference
Between heartbreak & a heart attack
Already lost to depression once
& I swear I'm not going back
But I can't do this alone anymore
I need you back in my life, man!
Damn.

Love Letter to My Ex(es)

Hey gorgeous,
You were my
First college romance
Well, more like a
Romantic tragedy
& it took me 6 years
To finally see that the
Executive director
Of our tragedy... was me

See, you & me
Could've went the distance
That's the truest story ever told
But hurt people, hurt people
& those are the truest words
I've ever wrote

In a relationship like ours
People never see the process,
Only the progress...
& eventually the demise
A lot like how I never saw
The pain I caused
Until you showed me
The river of tears
Flowing down your eyes.

Hey beautiful,
You were the
Perfect girlfriend
Always so dutiful
There was honestly
Nothing more I EVER
Should've asked of you

You were also
The cheerleader type
I always wanted to date
Back in high school
But back in those days
I was the LAST guy
Anyone would've thought
Was cool enough
To date you…
But eventually I did &
Faster than the speed of love
From your affection, I hid
A dark part of me
Learned to find
Peace of mind
In your uncertainty
Turns out you were also
The perfect girlfriend
To misplace the blame
For trying to hurt me.

Hey love,
Told you I'd write

Something about us
Even I didn't think
It would be so soon
But how can I forget
The first time
You ever came to my room?

I was shaking in my boots
Awkward silence
Loud as a sonic boom
Almost as loud as
The silence from
My voice of empathy
On the days
Leading up to our doom

Even after all the
Valleys we trekked & hills we climbed
I STILL reserved my right
Not to take the inconvenient truth
As a sign
So instead I chose to rationalize
More self-consoling lies
With yet another, "Maybe next time."

This is a love letter to my ex(es)
Signed by a man who
Never thought I deserved to be loved
Convinced myself emotions
Just weren't for me

Like OJ Simpson
& the murderous glove
So instead I chose to drown
In my pool of misery
& refused to let ANY of you
Swim close enough
To try & rescue me
Because I was a REAL man
...or, at least, so I thought
So I folded every card
That was dealt to me
In matters of the heart

It took me a while to understand
I was afraid to take a chance
Like closing my eyes
Before I rolled the dice
It took me even longer
To understand that
TRUE love equals TRUE sacrifice
Like the left lung being smaller
To make your heart fit right

& most importantly
It took me a while to see
That through every
Failed relationship in my wake
& every time I promised myself,
"This time it will be a piece of cake"
& every time I ignored the sound
Of your heartbreak, for my own sake

Nothing ever changed
Our outcome was always the same
Because the only thing
That ever needed to change...
Was me.

Y3b3hyia Bio (Final Farewell)

Landed at Kotoka Int'l
July 27
Took my first breath of air
Could've swore I was in heaven
So I stepped off the plane
Searching the crowd for a reverend
But instead I found Auntie Rose,
Which was even better!

Spent the first few weeks
Just getting my head together
Learning to digest the food
& dressing right for the weather

But what's really wild is
Even my wildest, dreams
Didn't prepare me
For what I've, seen here
Uninhibited expression
Even grown men smile
From ear to ear
It's memories like those
That fill me with fear
Dreading each day
The end of my stay
Creeps near

Throughout this journey
I've racked up about...
4,000 frequent flyer miles
Ate waakye & shito
Like they were going out of style
Found out Commonwealth
Wasn't so common after all
Even smuggled a bookcase at 4am
From ISH to Volta Hall

& how can I forget
Watching our Black Stars
Go for the win
In the 2015
African Cup of Nations?
Their loss broke my heart
Like a handful of 50s
From the ATM

But on a serious note,
I met some incredible
Human beings
Whose relationships
I hope last a while
& speaking of relationships,
I was in & out of one
Faster than the
Change of a radio dial
But I don't mind
Because through it all,
I smile :)

I smile because,
Ghana taught me
Not to be ashamed
To walk tall
Ghana taught me
That it's okay
To want it all
Ghana taught me
There's a thin line
Between right & wrong
Ghana taught me
That every soul sings
A special song

One day I'll reflect
On these lessons
& be so proud
But by that time I'll be
Speaking to
1,000 people in a crowd!

Ok, that may be
A bit of an exaggeration
But Ghana also taught me
Not to pre-package my dreams
With hesitation
So much more to say,
But I'm running out of
Time to say it
So here it is, the finale

In summation...
On the day I leave Ghana
I will be reborn
From this womb I've known 9 months
I will be torn
Back into the land of hypocrisy...
I mean, the land of "the free"
I will be sworn
With a suitcase full of memories
For my loved ones to adorn

In all honesty I have
No idea how to end this
But looking back,
I had no idea
How to begin this
Maybe that's because
I still can't fathom
Being allowed to bear witness
To such a life-changing decision
I know in my soul that
Nothing will be the same
After this

So needless to say,
Your beautiful faces
I'll surely miss
Medaase paa
To each & every one of you
(Even white Jesus)

& last, but not least,
To Mother Ghana dearest
I hope you've learned
As much from me
As I have from you
Only time will tell,
I know,
I don't want to leave
But I HAVE to go
So until next time...
Y3b3hyia bio.